South American Animals

Toucans

ABDO
Publishing Company

Big Buddy BOOKS
South American Animals

by Julie Murray

VISIT US AT
www.abdopublishing.com

Published by ABDO Publishing Company, PO Box 398166, Minneapolis, Minnesota 55439.

Printed in the United States of America, North Mankato, Minnesota.
092013
012014

 PRINTED ON RECYCLED PAPER

Coordinating Series Editor: Rochelle Baltzer
Editor: Marcia Zappa
Contributing Editors: Megan M. Gunderson, Bridget O'Brien, Sarah Tieck
Graphic Design: Maria Hosley
Cover Photograph: *Shutterstock*: Eduardo Rivero.
Interior Photographs/Illustrations: *Getty Images*: Visuals Unlimited, Inc./Gregory Basco (p. 23), Luciano Candisani (p. 19), Frans Lemmens (p. 15), Pete Oxford (p. 27), Panoramic Images (p. 23), Christine und JÂrgen Sohns (p. 12), Art Wolfe (p. 21); *Glow Images*: Glenn Bartley (p. 7), Ritterbach (p. 29), SuperStock (p. 17); *iStockphoto*: ©iStockphoto.com/jokos78 (p. 8), ©iStockphoto.com/mlpeck (p. 13) ©iStockphoto.com/ranplett (p. 9), ©iStockphoto.com/JohanSjolander (p. 4); *Minden Pictures*: © ZSSD (p. 25); *Science Source*: Steve Cooper (p. 15); *Shutterstock*: david alayo (p. 9), Ammit Jack (p. 4), Pablo H Caridad (p. 5), Steve Herrmann (p. 7), Krzysztof Wiktor (p. 11).

Library of Congress Cataloging-in-Publication Data

Murray, Julie, 1969- author.
 Toucans / Julie Murray.
    pages cm. -- (South American animals)
 Audience: 7 to 11.
 ISBN 978-1-62403-194-6
1. Toucans--Juvenile literature. I. Title.
QL696.P57M87 2014
598.7'2--dc23
                                2013025496

Contents

Amazing South American Animals 4

Toucan Territory 6

Welcome to South America! 8

Take a Closer Look 10

A Bill to Behold 14

Forest Life 18

Mealtime 22

Baby Toucans 24

Survivors 28

Wow! I'll bet you never knew... 30

Important Words 31

Web Sites 31

Index 32

Long ago, nearly all land on Earth was one big mass. About 200 million years ago, the land began to break into **continents**. One of these is South America.

Toucans are famous for their big, bright bills.

South America includes several countries and **cultures**. It is known for its rain forests and interesting animals. One of these animals is the toucan.

Toucan Territory

There are about 40 different types of toucans. They live in much of South America and Central America. Central America is the southern part of North America.

Most toucans live in **tropical** rain forests. These forests are warm, wet, and thick with plants. Some toucans live in cooler forests.

Toucan Territory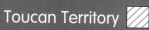

Uncovered!
Toucans are closely related to woodpeckers.

Some small types of toucans are called toucanets or aracaris. These include the crimson-rumped toucanet (*left*) and the chestnut-eared aracari (*right*).

Welcome to South America!

If you took a trip to where toucans live, you might find...

...soaring mountains.

Some toucans live on the slopes of the Andes Mountains. This mountain system runs about 5,500 miles (8,900 km) down South America's west side. Its highest peak is Mount Aconcagua, at about 22,830 feet (6,960 m).

SOUTH
PACIFIC
OCEAN

SOU

Strait of Magellan

Cape Horn

...football.

The most popular sport in South America is football, or soccer. *Futbitol*, or little football, is also popular. It is similar to football, but played on a smaller field.

Cape of Good Hope

...the Amazon rain forest.

South America is home to the world's largest tropical rain forest. The Amazon is in northern South America. It has many different animals and plants. The plants in the Amazon grow in layers. Toucans usually live in the top layer, which is called the canopy.

Take a Closer Look

Toucans have oval bodies, thick necks, and small heads. They have strong legs and short, rounded wings. A toucan's tail is long.

Toucans are covered in feathers. Different types of toucans have different colored feathers. Many have black or green feathers on their bodies. They have white, blue, yellow, orange, or red feathers on their faces, throats, and chests.

Toucans have two toes that point forward and two that point backward. This helps them hold tight and balance when standing on branches.

Different types of toucans range widely in size. Adults can be from 10 to 25 inches (25 to 64 cm) long. They can weigh from 3.5 to 30.5 ounces (99 to 865 g).

The largest type of toucan is the toco toucan.

One of the smallest types of toucans is the green aracari.

A Bill to Behold

Toucans are known for their showy bills. They may be black, brown, blue, green, red, yellow, or white. Many toucans have bills with several colors.

Some toucans have bills that are nearly as long as their bodies! More often, they are about one-third of their body length. Even though a toucan's bill is very large, it is lightweight. That is because it is mostly hollow, with thin bones for support.

Uncovered!
Scientists believe bill colors help different types of toucans tell each other apart.

A toucan's bill is made of keratin. Keratin also makes up fingernails and hair.

Many types of toucans are named for their bills. The yellow-ridged toucan has a yellow stripe on the top of its bill.

Scientists have several ideas about what a toucan uses its bill for. A toucan may use its large bill to reach faraway food. Or, it may use it to keep cool. As blood moves through the bill, heat escapes.

A toucan may also use its large bill to **protect** itself. A toucan's bill isn't strong enough for fighting. But, its large size may scare away predators.

Uncovered!
Toucans have many predators. These include boars, jaguars, snakes, and large birds such as eagles and hawks. In addition, small animals such as rats and weasels eat toucan eggs.

Toucans use their long bills to reach food on branches that can't support their weight.

Forest Life

Toucans are **social** birds. They live in small groups called flocks. Flocks usually have about 2 to 12 members.

Toucans are noisy! Their call sounds include yelps, barks, croaks, and growls. In addition, toucans make noise by tapping and clattering their bills.

Toucans often move their heads, bills, and tails when they call.

Uncovered!

Toucans call to warn others about danger or lead them to food. A call also helps different types of toucans tell each other apart.

19

Toucans are generally found in the tops of trees. A toucan's rounded wings are not built for flying far. Luckily, toucans don't have to! They live in thick forests where they can hop between branches.

At night, most toucans rest in holes in trees. They find holes made by woodpeckers or broken branches. Sometimes, a whole flock of toucans sleeps in the same hole.

When a toucan sleeps, it turns its head around and rests its bill on its back. Then, it folds its wings and tail over its bill. Sleeping this way helps toucans fit in small holes.

Mealtime

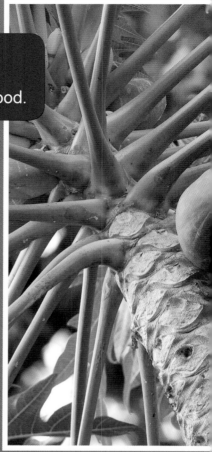

A toucan's bill has sharp, sawlike edges. This helps it tear apart large pieces of food.

Toucans are **omnivores**. This means they eat both plants and meat. Toucans mainly eat fruit, such as figs and wild cherries. But they also eat nuts, seeds, bugs, frogs, and lizards. Sometimes, they eat the babies and eggs of other birds.

A toucan grabs food with its bill. Then, it tosses its head back to throw the food into its mouth. It uses its long, feather-like tongue to guide food into its mouth.

Baby Toucans

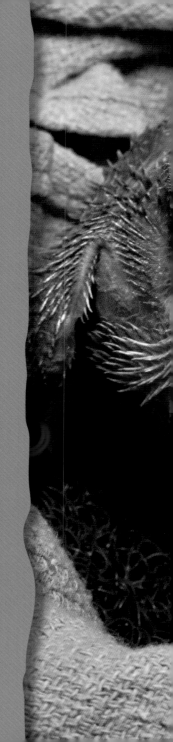

Most toucans **mate** once a year. Then, the female lays one to five eggs in a hole in a tree. Toucan eggs are shiny and white. The male and female take turns keeping them warm.

After 14 to 20 days, the eggs **hatch**. Newly hatched toucans are helpless. They are blind and featherless. They have small, soft bills.

Baby toucans are called chicks.

Both parents take care of toucan chicks. They feed them, clean their nest, and guard them from predators.

After about three weeks, chicks open their eyes and begin to grow feathers. Toucan chicks are ready to leave the nest after six to nine weeks.

A toucan chick's bill is usually full grown before it leaves the nest.

Survivors

Life in South America isn't easy for toucans. New buildings and farms take over their **habitats**. And because of their bright colors, people often capture them to sell as pets.

Still, toucans **survive**. People work to save their rain forest habitats. Toucans help make South America an amazing place.

In the wild, toucans live for up to 20 years.

Wow!
I'll bet you never knew...

...that toucans have been used to advertise products. That's because they are easily recognized. And, many people see them as being playful and smart.

...that the word *toucan* is based on a native Brazilian word, *tucana*. It came from a sound toucans make.

...that toucans are good for the rain forest. Toucans often eat fruit with seeds. When they poop, the seeds come out and sometimes grow into new plants!

Important Words

continent one of Earth's seven main land areas.

culture (KUHL-chuhr) the arts, beliefs, and ways of life of a group of people.

habitat a place where a living thing is naturally found.

hatch to be born from an egg.

mate to join as a couple in order to reproduce, or have babies.

omnivore (AHM-nih-vawr) an animal that eats both plants and meat.

protect (pruh-TEHKT) to guard against harm or danger.

social (SOH-shuhl) naturally living or growing in groups.

survive to continue to live or exist.

tropical of or relating to parts of the world where temperatures are warm and the air is moist all the time.

Web Sites

To learn more about toucans, visit ABDO Publishing Company online. Web sites about toucans are featured on our Book Links page. These links are routinely monitored and updated to provide the most current information available.

www.abdopublishing.com

Index

Aconcagua, Mount **8**

Amazon rain forest **9**

Andes Mountains **8**

bill **5, 14, 15, 16, 17, 18, 19, 21, 22, 23, 24, 27**

body **10, 11, 14, 19, 20, 21, 23**

Brazil **30**

Central America **6**

chestnut-eared aracari **7**

chicks **24, 25, 26, 27**

communication **18, 19, 30**

crimson-rumped toucanet **7**

dangers **16, 19, 26, 28**

eating habits **16, 17, 19, 22, 23, 30**

eggs **16, 24**

feathers **10, 24, 26**

flocks **18, 20, 26**

green aracari **13**

habitat **6, 9, 20, 28**

mating **24**

nest **26, 27**

predators **16, 26**

size **7, 12, 13, 14, 16, 17**

South America **4, 5, 6, 8, 9, 28**

toco toucan **13**

weather **6**

woodpeckers **7, 20**

yellow-ridged toucan **15**